THE
protein-packed
BREAKFAST CLUB

Easy High Protein Recipes with 300 Calories or Less to Help You Lose Weight and Boost Metabolism

Lauren Harris-Pincus, MS, RDN

Eggplant Press, a division of Beth Shepard Communications, LLC

http://www.bethshepard.com

Copyright © 2017
Text and Photographs by Lauren Harris-Pincus, MS, RDN
Cover art by Jared Pincus and Jordan Pincus
Cover recipe: Creamy Orange Overnight Oats- page 20
Nutrient analysis of recipes performed using ESHA Food Processor
All rights reserved.
ISBN-13: 978-1543011241
ISBN-10: 1543011241

NOTE TO THE READER

The information found in this book is intended to help guide you toward healthier eating choices, but is not intended as medical advice or to replace the services of a qualified medical professional. Consult your physician before adopting the suggestions in this book. Seek medical attention if you suspect that you have a health challenge.

Any mention of an organization, product, service, company, or professional does not imply endorsement by either the author or the publisher. Any adverse effect arising from the use or misuse of the information from this book is the sole responsibility of the reader and not that of the author or publisher. The author and the publisher disclaim any liability directly or indirectly from the use of the material in this book by any person.

DEDICATION

For my Grandma Lee (MiMi),

Your warm and loving kitchen was my happy place.

Thank you for always encouraging me to reach for the stars.

Miss you every day...

ACKNOWLEDGMENTS

The last thing I ever thought I would become is an author and I am so privileged for the opportunity to write and share this book with my readers and clients. Thank you to Melissa Joy Dobbins, MS, RD for sparking this idea and encouraging me to pursue it. Many thanks to Beth Shepard, my fantastic agent and friend for believing in me and guiding me so patiently through this very long process.

To my mom for having nutrition books lying around when I was a kid, for always being an inspiration in the kitchen and serving as my personal eager recipe tester, and to both you and dad for loving and supporting me unconditionally no matter my size.

To Julie: sisters are forever.

To my husband, Allan for nurturing my dream eggs and encouraging me to follow this exciting, windy path.

To my little loves, Jared and Jordan, the best teenage graphic design and video production team. Thank you for the always appreciated and much needed creative input and tech support! Also for putting up with my travel, late working nights, a seemingly endless stream of breakfast recipes coming out of the kitchen, and especially the semi-permanent food photography set up in our living room. Love you "infinite"!

ABOUT THE AUTHOR

Lauren Harris-Pincus, MS, RDN, is a nutrition communications specialist, speaker, spokesperson, corporate consultant and Registered Dietitian in private practice. She is the founder and owner of Nutrition Starring YOU, LLC where she specializes in weight management and prediabetes.

Formerly an obese child, Lauren dedicates herself to combating the growing adult and childhood obesity epidemic. She loves to play around in the kitchen creating waistline-friendly meals and developing recipes for corporate clients. Lauren holds both Bachelor of Science and Master of Science degrees in Nutrition from Penn State and New York University, respectively. She completed the dietetic internship program at The New York Hospital-Cornell Medical Center in NYC.

Lauren has been featured in U.S. News and World Report, The Huffington Post, Fox News, Shape, The New York Post, SELF, Fitness, Prevention, Men's Fitness, Brides, Everyday Health, Reader's Digest, Today's Dietitian and more. She is also a frequent guest on Sirius/XM radio.

Get social with Lauren:

Twitter: https://twitter.com/LaurenPincusRD

Instagram: https://www.instagram.com/laurenpincusrd/

Pinterest: http://www.pinterest.com/LaurenPincusRD/

Facebook: https://www.facebook.com/NutritionStarringYou

YouTube: https://www.youtube.com - search Lauren Pincus

INTRODUCTION

"One should not attend even the end of the world without a good breakfast."
— author, Robert A. Heinlein

Increasing protein in your diet is a current hot trend in the media and nutrition world, however so many people totally miss the opportunity to benefit from a protein-packed breakfast that would help to curb high and empty calorie snacking throughout the day. After 20 years working as a registered dietitian with thousands of nutrition clients, "What should I eat for breakfast?" is the most common question I am asked.

Most of us are not aware that the human body can only utilize about 25-30 grams (approximately 4 ounces) of protein at a time to maximize muscle building and repair (2). This is easy for us to consume when we indulge ourselves at dinner, however breakfast is often overlooked. The key is to spread your protein consumption throughout the day, starting with breakfast to maximize the body's natural protein processing power. Do you find yourself starving by 10 am after drinking coffee along with a giant bagel, or struggling to make it to lunch after sweetened cereal and a banana? Shifting your regimen to a high protein, nutrient-rich breakfast is a game changer. Additionally, every meal should contain a combination of protein, fats, fiber and "good" carbohydrates. Not only does this support weight loss and sustained energy levels, this also helps to preserve and build muscle mass— an important part of supporting a healthy metabolism (1,3). When you discover the tools to start your day with a proper breakfast, your whole relationship with food will improve. Balanced nutrition is the key, and starting your day with a protein-packed breakfast is critical.

Whether for weight loss, managing prediabetes or Type II diabetes, or a healthy, fit lifestyle, **The Protein-Packed Breakfast Club** is filled with over 30 delicious, easy to make recipes that are each 300 calories or less and packed with a minimum of 20 grams of protein. Many recipes you will find online boast a high protein content, but may contain upwards of 700 calories to achieve it. Anyone looking to watch portion sizes while achieving weight management and blood sugar goals will find these recipes can fit well into your lifestyle.

But I have no time, you say? Well, I have the solution for that! By design, most recipes can be made ahead of time, not while rushing out the door to work or school. Spending a few minutes at night or on the weekend preparing your morning meal can make all the difference in the world to your overall health, and is sure to improve your day.

From dairy, to protein powders, nuts, seeds, eggs and ancient grains, there is something for everyone, I promise! I've included hot trends like overnight oats, smoothie bowls and mug cakes that are flooding social media. Many recipes are vegetarian and gluten free to accommodate the increasing number of people who eliminate gluten from their diets.

These recipes contain protein, whole grain carbs, fiber and healthy fats which delay digestion and can prevent a rise and the resulting crash in blood sugar. It's become quite apparent in our increasingly hectic lives that taking the time to cook a high protein, nutrient rich breakfast is becoming harder and harder, even though meals like this sustain your energy levels much longer. I'll show you how to do it so that you can easily incorporate these recipes into your routine for yourself and your family. I purposefully duplicated ingredients many times throughout the book to allow you to make several recipes within a week after one shopping trip. One container of cottage cheese, ricotta cheese, yogurt, etc., can be used to prepare several days' worth of recipes.

So come along, join the club — **The Protein-Packed Breakfast Club!**

Important ingredient tips and tricks to help make the most delicious recipes:

1. A few things to keep in mind when choosing a no-calorie sweetener:
There is much debate in the media and the scientific community about the safety and effectiveness of artificial sweeteners. I'm an "all foods can fit" type of person and you may use whichever sweetener you prefer to achieve your desired result. For reference, I developed these recipes with **stevia or monkfruit** because they are considered natural" sweeteners by the FDA and meet my taste preference.

2. Not all brands and varieties provide equal levels of sweetness per serving.
Most individual packets are standardized to <u>equal the sweetness of 2 teaspoons of sugar.</u> However, some are measure for measure with sugar which means you would likely need 2 packets to achieve the same sweetness as others. Read the label and determine the amount you need.

3. Different brands of sweeteners use several types of bulking agents which affects the taste, texture and calories.
Since the main ingredient in products like stevia, sucralose, aspartame, etc., is likely hundreds of times sweeter than sugar, you would need so little that packaging it alone would be impractical. Some manufacturers use bulking agents such as dextrose (a sugar), or maltodextrin (a starch) which are usually about 1 gram which provides 4 calories. No big deal for 1 packet but if using several in your meal or many more in a recipe, the carbs and calories can add up. Erythritol is a sugar alcohol which contains zero calories and even though you may see a couple grams of carbs on the label, it's not absorbed so it does not provide calories. Also, in most people, erythritol does not cause GI symptoms unlike sorbitol or other sugar alcohols. If you've ever eaten too much sugar free candy and felt tummy distress, that's why. There should be no issues with erythritol.

4. Packets and bags of the same brand of sweetener are not necessarily the same:
If purchasing a "spoonable" sweetener in a larger container or bag, check the serving size to see if it's "measure for measure" with sugar. In that case, you would require 2 teaspoons to equal the sweetness of 1 packet in my recipes. One mainstream spoonable brand measures 3/4 teaspoon to equal the sweetness of 2 teaspoons sugar. Read the label!

5. Everyone has their own sense of "sweet tooth".

When I ask clients how they take their coffee, the answers vary tremendously. Some like it black, others with cream and 5 packets of sweetener. I created these recipes to fall somewhere in the middle of the sweetness spectrum. Therefore, you may want to increase or decrease the amount of sweetener you use. Just remember, if you make a recipe and think it's not sweet enough, just add a little extra and vice versa.

Ingredient Tips:

How to choose a protein powder:

Whey protein powder is my favorite because it tastes the best and contains the highest amount of protein for the fewest calories. I chose a whey protein with very few ingredients and stevia as the sweetener. The variety used in these recipes provides 20 grams of protein per scoop for 90 calories. If you cannot find a similar product or they are out of your price range, don't worry. Other options will still work well, though you may be consuming a few extra calories in order to achieve the same amount of protein. I've chosen to include recipes featuring vanilla, chocolate and coconut flavored whey protein.

If you prefer a plant-based protein, there are several on the market with similar calorie to protein ratios. They add a bit of a "woodsy" flavor so if you like that, you can certainly switch things up. One thing to note is that plant-based protein powders tend to absorb more liquid than whey so you may have to adjust the recipes when making that substitution, especially if letting it sit overnight.

The one type of recipe that works significantly better with plant-based protein powders are mug cakes. Whey protein will yield a much tougher, drier cake so stick with a vegan protein powder for a moister mug cake.

Chia and flax seeds:

I love chia and flax because they are plant-based sources of protein, fiber and omega 3 fatty acids. In recipes, they absorb liquid and provide bulk and satiety. If you don't have chia seeds and choose to make a recipe such as a smoothie bowl or overnight oats, reduce the liquid or you'll end up with a thinner product. Plus, if you leave them out you may become hungry more quickly.

Cottage Cheese:
Though seemingly simple, there are so many varieties of cottage cheese and a plethora of ingredients they may contain. I use low fat (1 or 2%) with 90 calories per 1/2 cup serving and a very limited ingredient list. Some brands use starches and fillers which increases the carbohydrate count and decreases the protein per serving. Look for a minimum of 13 grams of protein per 1/2 cup for 90 calories. One of the mainstream brands only contains 10 grams- if you use that one the protein content of these recipes will be lower than what I've analysed.

Nut Milks
Most of my recipes call for unsweetened vanilla almond milk which contains 25-30 calories per cup with 0 grams of sugar vs 12 grams in standard dairy milk. I chose this because I'd rather balance the carbohydrate content of the meals with whole grains or fruit while keeping the total carbs and calories in check. Most recipes will work with any flavor nut milk as long as it's <u>unsweetened</u> like coconut, almond or cashew. Also, make sure they are fortified with calcium, one national brand is very low while others contain 45% of the daily value of calcium per cup.

Kitchen Must-Haves:
There are a few key items that will make preparing the Protein-Packed Breakfast Club recipes a breeze. Take a look at the food photos for ideas for serving bowls and jars as well. Everything tastes better in a pretty bowl :-)

A small whisk- perfect for blending protein powder into recipes
Ramekins- approximately 8-10 ounces
Mason jars- 12-16 ounces
A wide, flat-bottomed mug (for mug cakes and flax muffins in a mug)
A zester or microplane
Foil muffin tin liners
4 cup glass measuring cup
Assorted measuring cups and spoons

TABLE OF CONTENTS

Chapter 1
OATS AND OATMEAL

Mocha Chip Overnight Oats - 16
Cranberry Walnut Overnight Oats - 18
Creamy Orange Overnight Oats - 20
Kiwi Lime Coconut Overnight Oats - 22
Apple Cinnamon Protein Oatmeal - 24
Pomegranate Coconut Oatmeal - 26
Peanut Chip Breakfast Cookie Dough - 28

Chapter 2
SMOOTHIES AND BOWLS

Chocolate Peanut Butter Smoothie - 32
Apple Peanut Butter Protein Smoothie - 34
Pumpkin Maple Walnut Smoothie Bowl - 36
Orange Cream Smoothie Bowl - 38
Pear Pistachio Smoothie Bowl - 40

Chapter 3
MUG CAKES, PANCAKES, FRENCH TOAST AND MORE

Triple Chocolate Mug Cake - 44
PB and Banana Mug Cake - 46
Pumpkin Ricotta Protein Pancakes - 48
Apple Cinnamon Protein Pancakes - 50
Cherry Vanilla French Toast - 52
Pumpkin Flax Muffin in a Mug - 54
Banana Walnut Bread Pudding in a Mug - 56

Chapter 4
EXCELLENT EGGS

Cheesy Egg Soufflés - 60
Sunny Eggs over Avocado Toast - 62
Bacon, Egg and Cheese Breakfast Sandwich - 64
Cheesy Egg and Flax Muffins - 66
Spinach, Egg White and Feta Wrap with Sun-dried Tomatoes - 68

Chapter 5
FUN WITH FRUIT, ANCIENT GRAINS AND CEREAL

Berries and Cream Filled Protein Crepes - 71
Pomegranate Strawberry Sorghum Parfait - 74
Chocolate Cherry Breakfast Ice Cream - 76
Raspberry Coconut Protein Cereal Bowl - 78
Banana, Yogurt and Cereal Bowl - 80
Clementine Cranberry Overnight Cereal Bowl - 82

Chapter 6
SAVORY TOAST AND WRAPS

Spicy Sausage over Avocado Toast - 86
Smoked Salmon Wrap - 88

Chapter 1:
OATS AND OATMEAL

When most people tell me they eat oatmeal for breakfast, they don't mean "real" oatmeal. They are referring to the processed, pre-sweetened microwavable packets full of sugar, salt and other potentially undesirable ingredients. What if I told you that you could enjoy oatmeal without cooking it? Or, incorporate it into recipes prepared in advance to allow you to reap the wonderful health benefits of oatmeal without taking time out of your busy morning routine? This chapter contains some of my favorite ways to enjoy oatmeal— mostly prepared ahead of time!

If you have never tried "**Overnight Oats**", they are life changing. The simple combination of old fashioned oats, some form of milk (dairy or non-dairy) and Greek yogurt is the base for an endless array of flavor combinations you can make at night and grab-and-go in the morning. If you prefer, you can heat it as well but there are no rules. Eat it how you like it. Protein-packed and satisfying, you may add almost any topping you can dream of while benefitting from the filling and heart-healthy soluble fiber in the oats. Also included here are ideas to power up your oatmeal bowl incorporating protein powder, fruit, nuts, coconut or whatever suits your fancy.

Oats 101: When to use different varieties

***Old Fashioned Oats:**
All my recipes are prepared with this standby. Most of us have the image of the tall blue canister of oatmeal in their mom's cupboard. Stick with these for maximum health benefit and hunger control. Research shows that consuming a serving of oats daily can help to lower the LDL or bad cholesterol, a nice bonus to your healthy breakfast.

*Quick oats cook faster, but are sliced and diced which means they take less effort to digest than old fashioned oats. They are less chewy and have a mushier texture. If that works for you, great, if not, stick with the old fashioned.

***Steel cut oats** are toasted and cut oat groats—the oat kernel that has been removed from the husk. They are extremely dense and require a longer cooking time, usually 20-30 minutes. Also, the portion size is small for the number of calories they contain. We are not using these here because of the nature of the recipes and cooking time.

Coffee in your oatmeal? Yup! Let's face it, most of us need our cup of morning coffee to get a jump start on our day. What if you could combine your cup of Joe with a delicious and healthy grab-and-go breakfast? This Mocha Overnight Oats recipe may become a new favorite. It's rich with the flavor of coffee and chocolate. You just might get hooked and save some dough from your morning coffee run.

MOCHA CHIP OVERNIGHT OATS – Makes 1 Serving

Ingredients:
1/3 cup old fashioned rolled oats
1/3 cup strong coffee, cooled
1/3 cup plain, nonfat Greek yogurt
1 packet stevia or preferred sweetener
3 Tablespoons chocolate whey protein powder
1 teaspoon chia seeds
1 teaspoon cocoa nibs or mini chocolate chips, divided

Instructions:
In a Mason jar or container with lid, add all ingredients and ½ teaspoon cocoa nibs or mini chips and stir.
Top with remaining 1/2 teaspoon cocoa nibs or chocolate chips.
Cover and refrigerate overnight.

Tip: For a deeper chocolate flavor, add ½ to 1 Tablespoon of unsweetened cocoa powder.

Mocha Chip Overnight Oats
Nutrition facts per serving: 260 calories, 6g total fat, 1.5g sat fat, 105mg sodium, 27g total carbohydrate, 5g dietary fiber, 6g sugars, 27g protein

Cranberries aren't just for Thanksgiving anymore. These antioxidant packed berries are a fantastic addition to your breakfast. If you usually don't prepare fresh cranberries, this recipe is so easy and since these treasures are naturally low in sugar, the whole recipe contains only 7 grams. The combo of sweet and tart flavors is a real pick-me-up in the morning.

CRANBERRY WALNUT OVERNIGHT OATS — Makes 1 Serving

Ingredients:
1 cup fresh cranberries
1 teaspoon lemon juice
1/2 teaspoon lemon zest
2 packets stevia or preferred sweetener
1/8 teaspoon cinnamon
1/3 cup old fashioned oats
1 teaspoon chia seeds
2 Tablespoons vanilla whey protein powder
1/2-1 packet stevia or preferred sweetener
1/3 cup unsweetened vanilla almond milk
1/3 cup plain, nonfat Greek yogurt
1 teaspoon chopped walnuts

Instructions:
Place cranberries in a glass or other microwave safe bowl, loosely cover and cook on high power for 2 to 2 1/2 minutes, until they burst and look juicy.
Stir in lemon juice, lemon zest, stevia and cinnamon.
Set aside to cool. Cover and refrigerate overnight.
In a separate Mason jar or container with a lid, add oats, chia seeds, protein powder, stevia, almond milk and yogurt and stir to combine.
Cover and refrigerate for a few hours or overnight.
When ready to serve, layer oat mixture with cranberries in a jar or parfait glass and top with walnuts.

Cranberry Walnut Overnight Oats
Nutrition facts per serving: 300 calories, 7g total fat, 1g sat fat, 140mg sodium, 37g total carbohydrate, 10g dietary fiber, 7g sugars, 25g protein

Thinking of Creamsicles brings back memories of hot summer days and running down the street after the ice cream truck. Now you can enjoy one of your childhood favorites in a healthier breakfast treat. You also benefit from 24 grams of satisfying protein and 80% of your recommended daily value of Vitamin C.

CREAMY ORANGE OVERNIGHT OATS — Makes 1 Serving

Ingredients:
1/3 cup old fashioned oats
1 teaspoon chia seeds
1 packet stevia or preferred sweetener
2 Tablespoons vanilla whey protein powder
1/4 cup unsweetened vanilla almond milk
2 Tablespoons orange juice
1/3 cup plain, nonfat Greek yogurt
1 teaspoon orange (clementine) zest
1 large clementine or mandarin orange, peeled and sectioned
1 teaspoon slivered almonds or hemp seeds

Instructions:
Add the first 4 dry ingredients to a container with a lid or Mason jar.
Mix well to combine.
Add the next 4 ingredients and mix well.
Add clementine slices and garnish with almonds or hemp seeds
Cover and refrigerate for several hours or overnight.
If you prefer to layer it like a parfait, leave off the clementine and nuts/seeds and add in the morning.

Creamy Orange Overnight Oats
Nutrition facts per serving: 290 calories, 6g total fat, .5g sat fat, 125mg sodium, 37g total carbohydrate, 7g dietary fiber, 13g sugars, 24g protein

Kiwi and lime have such a tropical flavor, this breakfast will make you feel like you are relaxing on a balcony in the Caribbean. With a nice balance of tart and sweet, you'll want to make it again and again. Plus, kiwis are a fantastic source of Vitamin C providing 160% of your recommended daily intake in this refreshing dish.

KIWI LIME COCONUT OVERNIGHT OATS — Makes 1 Serving

Ingredients:
1/3 cup old fashioned oats
1 teaspoon chia seeds
2 Tablespoons vanilla or coconut whey protein powder
1 packet stevia or preferred sweetener
1/3 cup unsweetened coconut milk
1/3 cup plain, nonfat Greek yogurt
1/2 teaspoon lime zest
1 1/2 teaspoons lime juice
1 large kiwi about 3 ½ ounces (100g), peeled and diced

Instructions:
Add oats, chia, whey protein and stevia to a Mason jar or a container with a lid and stir.
Add coconut milk and stir.
Add Greek yogurt, lime juice and zest and stir to combine.
Gently stir in most of the diced kiwi, reserving some to add on top.
Cover and refrigerate for several hours or overnight.

Tip: Did you know you can scoop the flesh out of a kiwi without peeling it? You save time and keep more of your delicious kiwi.

Kiwi Lime Coconut Overnight Oats
Nutrition facts per serving: 300 calories, 7g total fat, 3g sat fat, 90mg sodium, 39g total carbohydrate, 8g dietary fiber, 12g sugars, 23g protein

This Apple Cinnamon Protein Oatmeal hits the spot on a cold, snowy morning. The down-home aroma and classic flavors are pure comfort food. The secret to protein-packed oatmeal is whisking together the protein powder with the milk to add in after cooking the oatmeal for a real stick to your ribs breakfast.

APPLE CINNAMON PROTEIN OATMEAL — Makes 1 Serving

Ingredients:
1 small apple, cored and diced (about 1 cup)
1/2 teaspoon cinnamon
1 Tablespoon water
1 packet of stevia or preferred sweetener, divided
1/2 cup old fashioned oats
3/4 cup water
dash kosher salt (1/16 teaspoon)
3 Tablespoons vanilla whey protein powder
1/4 cup unsweetened vanilla almond milk (or milk of choice)
1/8 teaspoon vanilla
Optional: drizzle with 1/2 teaspoon maple syrup or sorghum syrup

Instructions:
Place diced apples in a glass or ceramic bowl. Add 1 Tablespoon of water and sprinkle with cinnamon.
Microwave on high for 3 minutes.
Remove from microwave, stir in 1/2 packet of sweetener and set aside.
In a large glass bowl or 1 quart glass measuring cup, add oats, 3/4 cup water and dash of salt.
Microwave for 2 minutes, 45 seconds.
While oatmeal is cooking, whisk together milk, protein powder, vanilla and remaining sweetener in a small bowl.
When oats are finished cooking, stir in milk mixture and 3/4 of the apples.
Transfer oatmeal to a serving bowl and top with remaining apples.
Drizzle with ½ teaspoon pure maple syrup, sugar free maple syrup or sorghum syrup if desired.

Apple Cinnamon Protein Oatmeal
Nutrition facts per serving: 300 calories, 3.5g total fat, .5g sat fat, 220mg sodium, 48g total carbohydrate, 8g dietary fiber, 15g sugars, 20g protein

A bowl of oatmeal is a wonderful way to up your whole grain intake and fill up on hearty breakfast. My hack to make this comfort food a high protein meal is to stir protein powder into some milk and add it to the already cooked oatmeal. This combo of coconut and pomegranate is delicious and takes your plain oatmeal to a new level without added sugars.

POMEGRANATE COCONUT OATMEAL — Makes 1 Serving

Ingredients:
1/2 cup old fashioned oats
3/4 cup water
dash salt
1/4 cup unsweetened vanilla almond milk or unsweetened coconut milk
1 packet stevia or preferred sweetener
3 Tablespoons vanilla or coconut whey protein powder
1/3 cup pomegranate seeds (arils)
1 Tablespoon unsweetened coconut flakes-divided

Instructions:
Add oats, water and salt into a large microwavable bowl or 4 cup glass measuring cup.
Microwave on high for 2 minutes and 45 seconds.
While oats are cooking whisk together milk, protein powder and sweetener in a small bowl.
Add milk mixture, most of the pomegranate seeds and 2 teaspoons of coconut to cooked oatmeal and stir.
Transfer to a serving bowl and garnish with a few remaining pomegranate seeds and 1 teaspoon coconut.

Pomegranate Coconut Oatmeal
Nutrition facts per serving: 310 calories, 8g total fat, 4g sat fat, 220mg sodium, 40g total carbohydrate, 7g dietary fiber, 9g sugars, 21g protein

Kids and adults alike enjoy a spoonful of cookie dough every now and then. Unfortunately, that comes with a risk of salmonella from raw eggs plus a ton of calories from fat and sugar. This Breakfast Cookie Dough provides the sweet and salty fun flavor combo you crave in a nutrient rich meal.

PEANUT CHIP BREAKFAST COOKIE DOUGH — Makes 1 Serving

Ingredients:
Cookie Dough:
1/2 cup plain, nonfat Greek yogurt
3 Tablespoons powdered peanut butter or peanut flour
1 packet stevia or preferred sweetener
1/8 teaspoon vanilla extract
2 Tablespoons old fashioned oats
2 teaspoons cacao nibs or mini chocolate chips

Toppings:
1 teaspoon chopped peanuts
1/2 teaspoon cacao nibs or mini chips

Instructions:
Combine cookie dough ingredients in a bowl and gently mix.
Top with chopped peanuts and remainder of cacao nibs/mini chips

Tip: This cookie dough can be made in advance though the oats will soften. If you like a chewier texture, prepare it when ready to enjoy your breakfast.

Peanut Chip Breakfast Cookie Dough
Nutrition facts per serving: 260 calories, 9g total fat, 2.5g sat fat, 190mg sodium, 27g total carbohydrate, 5g dietary fiber, 12g sugars, 22g protein

Chapter 2:
SMOOTHIES AND SMOOTHIE BOWLS

Smoothies and smoothie bowls are a fantastic way to increase the protein and produce in your breakfast. My secret ingredient when preparing smoothies or bowls is cottage cheese! It's high in protein, low in carbs and is less tart than Greek yogurt so you need less added sweetener in your smoothie. If you are not a fan of cottage cheese, don't worry! Once blended, the texture is smooth and you cannot tell it's in there.

Smoothie bowls make a terrific breakfast because you get to chew instead of simply sipping. There's something much more satisfying about topping a smoothie bowl with fruit, nuts, seeds or granola and eating with a spoon.
Most of these recipes can be made in the evening, covered and refrigerated. The product usually thickens overnight, especially if there's added chia seeds, flax or high fiber cereal and you don't need to do anything more to it in the morning, just enjoy. If you do prepare your smoothie bowl in advance and need to make it thicker, you can add the smoothie plus ice back to the blender if needed.

BONUS WEB RECIPE

Toasted Coconut Wild Blueberry Smoothie Bowl recipe available at www.NutritionStarringYOU.com

This Chocolate Peanut Butter Smoothie is my husband's favorite. In fact, he likes it so much, he's willing to make it for himself in the morning and take it to work in an insulated cup. Big win for me and he's starting the day with 10 grams of fiber and 31 grams of satisfying protein. And really, who doesn't love chocolate and peanut butter together?

CHOCOLATE PEANUT BUTTER SMOOTHIE — Makes 1 Serving

Ingredients:
1 cup unsweetened vanilla almond milk
1/4 cup chocolate whey protein powder
2 teaspoons chia seeds
3 Tablespoons powdered peanut butter or peanut flour
1/2 frozen banana, sliced
1/2 cup ice
If desired, garnish with a sprinkle of powdered peanut butter and cocoa powder.

Instructions:
Add all ingredients into a blender and process until desired consistency is achieved.

Tip: If you wish to lower the sodium content of the smoothie, look for a brand of powdered peanut butter without added sodium like Crazy Richard's.

Chocolate Peanut Butter Smoothie
Nutrition facts per serving: 290 calories, 9g total fat, 0g sat fat, 410mg sodium, 28g total carbohydrate, 10g dietary fiber, 9g sugars, 31g protein

Who doesn't love apples dipped in peanut butter? It's not only delicious, but a wholesome, nutritious snack filled with protein, fiber and healthy fats. Now you can enjoy your favorite snack for breakfast in the form of a protein-packed smoothie!

APPLE PEANUT BUTTER PROTEIN SMOOTHIE — Makes 1 Serving

Ingredients:
1/4 cup apple cider
2 Tablespoons unsweetened vanilla almond milk
1/3 cup low fat cottage cheese
1 teaspoon chia seeds
1/4 cup powdered peanut butter or peanut flour
1 Tablespoon old fashioned oats
1/2 teaspoon cinnamon
1 small-medium very ripe apple like Gala, Fuji, Honeycrisp or Autumn Glory, about 4 ounces
1/2 -1 cup ice

Instructions:
Add all ingredients to a blender and process until smooth.
Garnish with extra sprinkles of powdered PB, cinnamon and tiny chopped apples.
If you like a little more spice, add ½ teaspoon of pumpkin pie spice.

Tip: If you like a sweeter smoothie or if your apple is not super sweet, you may want to add a packet of stevia.

Apple Peanut Butter Protein Smoothie
Nutrition facts per serving: 300 calories, 7g total fat, 1.5g sat fat, 270mg sodium, 39g total carbohydrate, 10g dietary fiber, 24g sugars, 23g protein

Everything about this smoothie bowl resembles a crisp fall day from the pumpkin pie spice to the toasted walnuts. It's sweet, creamy, crunchy, and contains heart-healthy omega 3 fats along with more than 1/3 of your daily fiber needs. Now that's a good morning!

PUMPKIN MAPLE WALNUT SMOOTHIE BOWL — Makes 1 Serving

Ingredients:
1/3 cup low fat cottage cheese
1/4 cup pumpkin puree
2 Tablespoons unsweetened vanilla almond milk
1 teaspoon chia seeds
1/2 teaspoon pumpkin pie spice
2 Tablespoons vanilla whey protein powder
1/2 frozen medium banana, sliced
1 Tablespoon coconut flour or 1 1/2 Tablespoons old fashioned oats
1 1/2 packets stevia or preferred sweetener
1/2 cup ice

Garnish:
1 Tablespoon walnuts, chopped and toasted (about 6 grams)
1 teaspoon pumpkin seeds (pepitas)
1 teaspoon pure maple syrup, sugar free syrup or sorghum syrup

Instructions:
Blend all ingredients except garnish until desired consistency is achieved. You may need to scrape down the sides.
Pour into a serving bowl and top with walnuts, pumpkin seeds and syrup of choice.

Pumpkin Maple Walnut Smoothie Bowl
Nutrition facts per serving: 300 calories, 11g total fat, 3g sat fat, 330mg sodium, 32g total carbohydrate, 9g dietary fiber, 15g sugars, 24g protein

Did you ever have an Orange Julius as a kid? This Orange Cream Smoothie Bowl stirs up that strong memory for me. This might be my favorite smoothie bowl, I think I may have actually licked the bowl. The flavors mesh so well and you benefit from an extra nutritional punch from 180% of your daily vitamin C.

ORANGE CREAM SMOOTHIE BOWL — Makes 1 Serving

Ingredients:
1/2-1 teaspoon orange zest
1 medium orange, peeled and quartered (about 6 ounces)
1/3 cup low fat cottage cheese
2 Tablespoons low sugar orange juice
2 Tablespoons vanilla whey protein powder
1 Tablespoon ground flaxseed
1 packet stevia or preferred sweetener
1/4 teaspoon almond extract
1 1/2 cups ice
1/4 ounce almonds, crushed (about 6 almonds)

Instructions:
Zest the orange, peel it and cut a thin horizontal slice out of the middle to reserve for a garnish. Quarter the remaining pieces.
Add the cottage cheese, orange juice, protein powder, flax, stevia, almond extract, zest, orange pieces and ice to a blender and process until smooth.
Pour into a bowl and garnish with orange slice, extra zest and almonds.

Tip: A juicy orange will make the tastiest smoothie. My absolute favorite are Cara Cara oranges. Have you tried them?

Orange Cream Smoothie Bowl
Nutrition facts per serving: 280 calories, 8g total fat, 1.5g sat fat, 280mg sodium, 31g total carbohydrate, 6g dietary fiber, 20g sugars, 23g protein

Pears and pistachios are a perfect "pairing". The flavors and texture mesh well together to create a delicious breakfast. Even though pears are more of a winter fruit, I still love making smoothie bowls when the outdoor temperature dips, and this one with the brightness of lemon and ginger wakes me up in the morning.

PEAR PISTACHIO SMOOTHIE BOWL — Makes 1 Serving

Ingredients:
1/3 cup low fat cottage cheese
2 Tablespoons unsweetened vanilla almond milk
1/2 medium pear, quartered, plus a few slices for garnish
2 teaspoons lemon juice
1/8 teaspoon ground ginger
1 teaspoon chia seeds
2 Tablespoons vanilla whey protein powder
2 Tablespoons old fashioned oats
1/2 cup ice
10 pistachios, shelled and crushed

Instructions:
Place all ingredients except pistachios and a few pear slices into a blender and process until desired consistency is achieved.

Pour into a bowl and top with a few pear slices, pistachios and a sprinkle of ground ginger.

Serve immediately

Pear Pistachio Smoothie Bowl
Nutrition facts per serving: 260 calories, 7g total fat, 1.5g sat fat, 320mg sodium, 28g total carbohydrate, 7g dietary fiber, 12g sugars, 23g protein

Chapter 3:
MUG CAKES, PANCAKES AND FRENCH TOAST

Usually thought of as high-carb bombs, pancakes and French toast are generally not considered weight loss friendly foods. Not anymore! Now you can enjoy some favorite comfort foods that are not only delicious but protein and fiber packed.

If you've never made a mug cake, they are so much fun. It's a guilt free "dessert for breakfast" type feel with flavors like chocolate and peanut butter to satisfy your sweet tooth. I recommend using pasteurized eggs or egg whites in mug cakes because they are best when left a bit undercooked and we don't want any food poisoning to ruin your fun. Please note that overcooking them can leave you with a hockey puck and that's not a tasty way to start the day. Always start on the lower end of the cooking range, they will continue to cook a bit after removing them from the microwave and you can always cook them for a few more seconds if needed.

As for pancakes, I've significantly upped the protein while keeping the calories in check. Plus, since the "batter" base is made from eggs/white, bananas and oats, my pancakes are gluten free. The addition of fruit and ricotta means you need little to no syrup to help keep calories and sugars in check.

I discovered the secret to protein packed French toast: dip the bread in a mixture of egg AND Greek yogurt before cooking. It keeps the bread moist and adds much more protein into your breakfast than a traditional recipe. Experiment with different yogurt flavors and fruit toppings for endless possibilities.

BONUS WEB RECIPE

Blueberry Protein Pancakes recipe available at www.NutritionStarringYOU.com

Cake for breakfast? No problem when you make a protein-packed mug cake. Less than 2 minutes in the microwave and breakfast is served. Packed with 32 grams of protein, this gluten free fluffy cake is fun to cook and eat. No guilt here, just chocolaty goodness.

TRIPLE CHOCOLATE PROTEIN MUG CAKE — Makes 1 Serving

Ingredients:
nonstick spray
1 egg-preferably pasteurized
1/4 banana, mashed (1 ounce)
1 packet stevia or preferred sweetener
2 Tablespoons unsweetened almond, cashew or coconut milk
1 teaspoon light buttery spread
2 Tablespoons plain, nonfat Greek yogurt
3 Tablespoons chocolate plant-based (vegan) protein powder
1 Tablespoon white whole wheat flour or sorghum flour (if gluten free)
1 Tablespoon unsweetened cocoa powder
1/2 teaspoon baking powder
2 teaspoons mini chocolate chips, divided

Instructions:
Spray a wide bottomed mug or similarly sized microwavable bowl with nonstick spray (such as coconut oil spray) and set aside.
Beat egg in a medium bowl. Add mashed banana, stevia, milk, butter spread, Greek yogurt and stir.
Add remaining dry ingredients except chips and stir well to combine.
Fold in 1 teaspoon of the chocolate chips
Pour batter into mug/bowl and microwave on high for approximately 1:30-1:45 until the top is slightly shiny/wet looking but mostly dry. (Do not overcook, it will continue to cook a bit once done.)
Once cake is done, top with remaining teaspoon of chocolate chips and stir to break up in the mug. The slightly wet top will absorb when stirred. Cake will be moist.

Tip: Using whey protein powder in a mug cake will yield a much drier product. The recipe will still work with whey protein but take care not to overcook it.

Triple Chocolate Mug Cake
Nutrition facts per serving: 280 calories, 10g total fat, 3g sat fat, 360mg sodium, 25g total carbohydrate, 4g dietary fiber, 10g sugars, 27g protein

PB and bananas is a timeless classic thanks to Elvis Presley. Add a modern spin by melding these fabulous flavors into a mug cake. With 33 grams of protein and only 8 grams of sugar this breakfast rocks. The drizzle of natural peanut butter and bananas on top is the winning combo. Enjoy!

PB AND BANANA PROTEIN MUG CAKE — Makes 1 Serving

Ingredients:
nonstick spray
1 egg
1/4 medium banana, mashed (1 ounce)
1 packet stevia or preferred sweetener
2 Tablespoons unsweetened almond, cashew or coconut milk
2 Tablespoons nonfat, plain Greek yogurt
3 Tablespoons vanilla plant-based (vegan) protein powder
2 Tablespoons powdered peanut butter or peanut flour
1/2 teaspoon baking powder

For topping:
1/2 ounce very thin banana slices (approximately 8 slices)
1 teaspoon natural peanut butter

Instructions:
Spray a wide bottomed mug or similarly sized bowl with nonstick spray.
Add egg and beat well.
Add mashed banana, stevia, milk, and yogurt, and stir until well combined.
Add remaining dry ingredients and stir well.
Microwave on high for approximately 1 minute and 45 seconds- until the top is slightly shiny/wet looking but mostly dry. (It will continue to cook a bit more once done.)
Break up the cake with a fork and top with banana slices and peanut butter

Tip: If using whey protein it will yield a drier, tougher product. Cook for approximately 1 minute and 30 seconds, (Do not overcook or it will get tough) The bottom will be slightly wet, use a fork to break up the cake and combine to even out the texture, the extra liquid will absorb.

PB and Banana Mug Cake
Nutrition facts per serving: 290 calories, 9g total fat, 1.5g sat fat, 450mg sodium, 19g total carbohydrate, 4g dietary fiber, 8g sugars, 33g protein

I'm always so temped to order pumpkin pancakes in a diner, yet I want to avoid the absurd number of calories they typically contain. Whip some up at home instead with this easy recipe you can make on a Sunday and keep on hand for a quick weekday breakfast. Thanks to canned pumpkin, you can enjoy this fall favorite all year long.

PUMPKIN RICOTTA PROTEIN PANCAKES — Makes 6 pancakes/2 Servings

Ingredients for Pancakes:
1 egg
2 egg whites or 1/4 cup plus 2 Tablespoons liquid egg whites
1/2 teaspoon vanilla extract
1/4 cup pumpkin puree
3/4 teaspoon pumpkin pie spice
1 medium very ripe banana, thoroughly mashed
1/2 cup old fashioned oats- blended into a flour

Topping
3/4 cup low fat or fat free ricotta cheese
1/4 cup pumpkin puree
2 packets stevia or preferred sweetener
1/4 teaspoon pumpkin pie spice
Garnish: 2 teaspoons pure or sugar free maple syrup

Instructions:
Beat egg and whites together in a medium bowl.
Add vanilla, pumpkin and pumpkin pie spice and whisk to combine.
Add mashed banana and whisk again. Add blended oats and stir well.
Spray a skillet or griddle with nonstick spray and heat on medium to medium high heat.
Use 1/4 cup to add batter to the skillet for each pancake, you may need to spread out batter with back of a spoon or spatula.
Flip carefully when bottom is golden brown- be patient. Remove when both sides are done.
Meanwhile, combine topping ingredients in a small bowl and set aside.
Layer 3 pancakes with 1/2 of ricotta mixture and sprinkle with extra pumpkin pie spice. Drizzle on syrup if desired.

Pumpkin Ricotta Protein Pancakes
Nutrition facts per serving: 300 calories, 4.5g total fat, 1g sat fat, 230mg sodium, 44g total carbohydrate, 7g dietary fiber, 20g sugars, 21g protein

Apple are such a cozy, down home food and what better way to feature them at breakfast than in pancakes? The ricotta topping adds a creamy decadence, extra sweetness and a protein boost as well.

APPLE CINNAMON PROTEIN PANCAKES — Makes 6 pancakes/2 Servings

Ingredients:
1 egg
1/4 cup plus 2 Tablespoons liquid egg whites
1 medium banana, mashed
1/2 cup old fashioned oats
1/2 teaspoon cinnamon
1/4 teaspoon vanilla extract
2 ounces (1/2 cup) apple cut into a small dice
2/3 cup low fat or fat free ricotta cheese
1-2 packets stevia or preferred sweetener
1-2 teaspoons lemon juice
Optional: sugar free or pure maple syrup

Instructions:
Beat egg and egg whites together in a medium bowl.
Add oats, cinnamon, vanilla and apples and stir to combine.
Spray a griddle or sauté pan with nonstick spray (I used coconut oil spray) and heat on medium to medium-high heat.
Drop batter by the 1/4 cupful into pan and flatten each pancake to cook more evenly.
Be patient and allow pancake to solidify before flipping.
Meanwhile, combine ricotta, lemon and stevia in a small bowl and set aside.
Remove pancakes from pan and divide into 3 pancake servings.
Top each serving with 1/4 cup ricotta mixture. Garnish with extra apple slices and cinnamon.

Apple Cinnamon Protein Pancakes
Nutrition facts per serving: 260 calories, 7g total fat, 2.5g sat fat, 210mg sodium, 35g total carbohydrate, 5g dietary fiber, 14g sugars, 19gprotein

French toast is such a staple brunch food. The trick to this protein-packed version is dipping the bread in egg plus Greek yogurt before cooking. Frozen cherries are a perfect topping because they produce juice when defrosted for a no sugar added syrup. Simply microwave them on the defrost setting or let sit in the refrigerator overnight before serving.

CHERRY VANILLA FRENCH TOAST — Makes 6 slices French toast/2 servings

Ingredients:
1 egg
1 egg white or 3 Tablespoons liquid egg whites
1/2 teaspoon cinnamon
1 5.3 ounce container lower sugar vanilla Greek yogurt (divided)
6 slices "light" whole wheat or sprouted bread (40-55 calories per slice)
20 frozen cherries, defrosted overnight or in the microwave
Optional: sugar free or pure maple syrup

Instructions:
Beat egg, egg white, and cinnamon in a medium bowl.
Whisk in most of the yogurt, reserving a few Tablespoons for garnish later.
Heat a griddle or sauté pan on medium to medium high heat with nonstick spray (I used coconut oil spray)
Dip each slice of bread in the egg mixture and place in pan, flipping once lightly browned.
Transfer to a plate and cover to keep warm.
Add 3 slices of French toast to a plate, top with 1 Tablespoon of vanilla yogurt and 10 cherries with their juice. Add a touch of sugar free maple syrup if desired.

Cherry Vanilla French Toast
Nutrition facts per serving: 250 calories, 3g total fat, 1g sat fat, 350mg sodium, 39g total carbohydrate, 13g dietary fiber, 9g sugars, 22g protein

Flax is a plant-based superfood with protein, fiber and omega 3 fats all rolled into one versatile seed. This recipe is a totally different take on a muffin and using ground flaxseeds instead of flour packs nearly 1/2 of your daily fiber needs into one easy and tasty breakfast.

PUMPKIN FLAX MUFFIN IN A MUG — Makes 1 Serving

Ingredients:
1/4 cup ground flax meal
3/4 teaspoon baking powder
3/4 teaspoon cinnamon
1/2 teaspoon pumpkin pie spice
2 packets stevia or preferred sweetener
1 Tablespoon vanilla whey protein powder
1 egg
1 teaspoon light whipped butter or other light buttery spread
1/2 teaspoon vanilla extract
2 Tablespoons pumpkin puree
2 Tablespoons lower sugar vanilla Greek yogurt, divided
1/2 teaspoon pumpkin seeds for garnish

Instructions:
In a mixing bowl combine first 6 dry ingredients and stir well.
Add egg, butter, vanilla, pumpkin and 1 Tablespoon of vanilla yogurt. Mix well.
Spray a flat, wide bottomed mug or large ramekin with cooking spray (I used coconut oil spray).
Pour in batter and flatten out the top.
Cook for 1:30 to 2 minutes. Try the lower end first, stop when still slightly moist and let sit for a few minutes to complete cooking. (Overcooking will yield a tougher, denser product)
To serve, top with remaining tablespoon of vanilla yogurt, extra pumpkin pie spice and a few pumpkin seeds if desired.

Pumpkin Flax Muffin in a Mug
Nutrition facts per serving: 290 calories, 16g total fat, 2.5g sat fat, 410mg sodium, 19g total carbohydrate, 12g dietary fiber, 3g sugars, 21g protein

When I hear bread pudding, I think of something too gooey and decadent to eat on a regular basis. Now you can enjoy some every day with this version of Banana Bread Pudding. Toasted walnuts add a fantastic depth of flavor and even though people think of bananas as super sweet, you're only consuming 8 grams of sugar in the whole meal. If you don't have or don't like sugar free syrup, one teaspoon of pure maple syrup will only add 17 calories and just over 4 grams of sugar.

BANANA WALNUT BREAD PUDDING IN A MUG — Makes 1 Serving

Ingredients:
1 egg
2 Tablespoons unsweetened vanilla almond milk
2 Tablespoons vanilla whey protein powder
1/2 teaspoon cinnamon
1 packet stevia or preferred sweetener
1/2 small-medium banana, mashed (2 ounces)
2 slices "light" whole wheat bread- 40-50 calories per slice, cut into 1/2 inch cubes

Garnish:
3 thin slices banana
1 Tablespoon chopped walnuts, toasted in toaster oven on foil for 2 ½ to 3 minutes
1 teaspoon sugar free maple syrup

Instructions:
Whisk together first 6 ingredients in a microwave safe mug until thoroughly combined.
Fold in the bread, gently stirring to coat with egg mixture.
Microwave on high for 1 minute, stir and cook another minute until set.
Garnish with banana, extra cinnamon, toasted walnuts and maple syrup.

Tip: To make in advance: Add egg mixture and bread to a mug, cover and refrigerate overnight.
Cook for 1 minute, stir and cook an additional 1 ½ minutes. Add toppings and serve. This works the best with bread that is on the way to stale.

Banana Walnut Bread Pudding in a Mug
Nutrition facts per serving: 300 calories, 10g total fat, 2g sat fat, 290mg sodium, 33g total carbohydrate, 9g dietary fiber, 8g sugars, 24g protein

Chapter 4:
EXCELLENT EGGS

Eggs are the quintessential breakfast protein and we all know they are very satisfying. The good news is that recent research has shown that the cholesterol in eggs is not a contributor to high cholesterol and heart disease. Woo-hoo! And, there are some wonderful nutrients and protein in the egg yolk that you don't want to ditch. Egg yolks are an excellent source of choline and selenium as well as a good source of vitamin D, B12, phosphorus and riboflavin. And in the spirit of the protein conversation, one egg provides 600 mg of leucine, an essential amino acid that is very important in building muscle protein! To keep the calories in check, I often combine eggs and egg whites in a recipe so you benefit from the nutrition, texture and color of the yolk without too many extra calories.

Make sure to pair these tasty egg dishes with some fruit or veggies to add extra nutrients and fiber if they are not already part of the recipe. Also, I like to use pasteurized eggs when I know I am leaving the yolk "runny" to avoid any chance of picking up salmonella. The risk is small but for the elderly or those with compromised immune systems, it's an easy way to eliminate any chance of infection. If not, you can always cook the yolk until it's no longer runny. It's a personal choice.

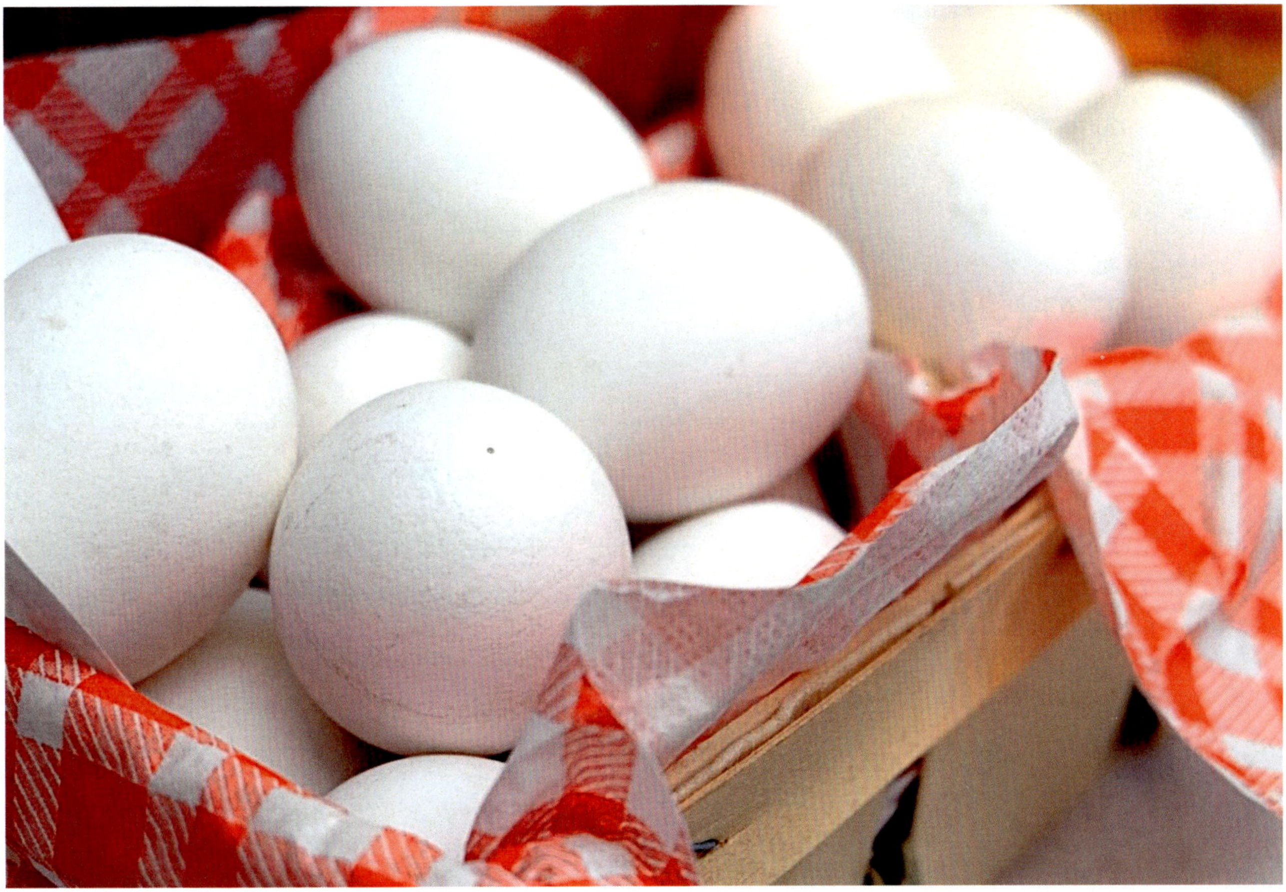

These adorable soufflés are very simple and tasty! I make a batch on the weekend for my husband to take to work on weekday mornings. Serve them with some whole grain toast and fruit for a well-rounded meal and added fiber. You can cover and refrigerate them for a quick microwavable breakfast all week long.

CHEESY EGG SOUFFLES — Makes 4 Servings

Ingredients:
2 eggs
1/4 cup plus 2 Tablespoons liquid egg whites
1 cup low fat cottage cheese
1 cup 2% (reduced fat) shredded Mexican blend or cheddar cheese, divided
2 Tablespoons chopped scallions (about 2 thin scallions)

Instructions:
Preheat oven or toaster oven to 350 degrees.
In a blender or food processor, combine egg, egg whites, cottage cheese and 1/2 of the shredded cheese and blend until thoroughly combined, approximately 30 seconds.
Lightly spray (4) 8-10 ounce ramekins with cooking spray. Pour 1/2 cup of egg mixture into each and sprinkle with remaining cheese and scallions.
Place ramekins on a baking sheet and bake for approximately 35-45 minutes until soufflés rise and are golden brown. If using a toaster oven, cook towards the lower end of the range.
Remove from the oven and serve. They will fall once out of the oven. Cover and refrigerate to reheat throughout the week.

Cheesy Egg Soufflés
Nutrition facts per serving: 170 calories, 10g total fat, 5g sat fat, 440mg sodium, 4g total carbohydrate, 0g dietary fiber, 2g sugars, 20g protein

If you have never paired eggs and avocado, I will show you the light. This breakfast is super filling and packed with protein, fiber and heart-healthy fats. If you don't have a fresh avocado available, simply substitute a few tablespoons of prepared guacamole.

SUNNY EGGS OVER AVOCADO TOAST — Makes 1 Serving

Ingredients:
2 eggs
2 Tablespoons liquid egg whites
2 slices "light" whole wheat bread, toasted (40-50 calories per slice)
1/3 avocado, mashed
Kosher salt and pepper to taste

Instructions:
Spray an omelet pan with nonstick spray and heat on medium to medium high heat. Crack the 2 eggs and add whites into the pan. Cook until the whites have set, flipping over if desired.
Meanwhile, toast the bread to your desired darkness.
Place toast on a plate and spread the mashed avocado on both slices.
Top with the eggs and a dash of kosher salt and pepper.

Tip: Add red pepper flakes or Sriracha for a little extra heat and garnish with cherry tomatoes.

Sunny Eggs over Avocado Toast
Nutrition facts per serving: 300 calories, 15g total fat, 4g sat fat, 350mg sodium, 21g total carbohydrate, 8g dietary fiber, 1g sugars, 23g protein

Breakfast sandwiches are popping up on every fast food menu, they are so popular that the largest chains are making them available all day. What makes this yummy meal unique is the slightly runny egg. The richness of the yolk is decadent and satisfying, yet the whole sandwich is perfectly balanced to keep you energized all morning.

BACON, EGG AND CHEESE BREAKFAST SANDWICH — Makes 1 Serving

Ingredients:
1 multigrain high fiber English muffin, toasted
1 wedge light spreadable Swiss cheese
2 slices turkey bacon (preferably uncured)
1 egg
black pepper to taste

Instructions:
Toast English muffin to desired darkness, spread one half with cheese wedge.
Spray a large nonstick pan with cooking spray and heat to medium-medium high heat.
Add turkey bacon on one side and egg on the other. It's easiest to use something to contain the egg like a round silicon mold or the cap of a Mason jar.
Turn bacon when browned on one side and cook until desired crispness.
Cook egg until the white is set and yolk is still slightly runny.
Add bacon and egg to English muffin, top egg with pepper to taste.

Tip: The turkey bacon featured in this recipe is uncured and contains 35 calories and 6 grams of protein per slice.
Add a slice of fresh tomato if you have some on hand for a little veggie boost.

Bacon, Egg and Cheese Breakfast Sandwich
Nutrition facts per serving: 280 calories, 11g total fat, 2.5g sat fat, 890mg sodium, 27g total carbohydrate, 9g dietary fiber, 3g sugars, 26g protein

While many love a sweet breakfast, sometimes savory just hits the spot. These protein-rich muffins are filled with cheesy, eggy goodness. Grab two with a piece of fruit to hit your AM protein goals or pair one with some scrambled eggs. I love having one crumbled atop my Cheesy Egg Soufflé recipe.

CHEESY EGG AND FLAX MUFFINS — Makes 8 Servings
Serving size 1 muffin

Ingredients:
2/3 cup low fat cottage cheese
1/4 cup grated Pecorino-Romano or Parmesan cheese
1/4 cup white whole wheat flour
2/3 cup flaxseed meal
1 teaspoon baking powder
3 eggs
3 tablespoons water
1/2 cup reduced fat (2%) shredded Mexican blend or cheddar cheese
2 Tablespoons fresh chives, chopped

Instructions:
Preheat oven to 400°F.
In mixing bowl, combine cottage cheese, Pecorino-Romano/Parmesan, flour, flaxseed meal, baking powder, eggs, and water.
Mix until well combined, then gently stir in shredded cheese and chives. Spray muffin tins with non-stick spray, or add foil muffin cups. Divide batter between eight muffin cups.
Bake muffins for 20 minutes or until lightly browned on top and set.
Make sure to cool completely before removing foil liners to prevent sticking.

Cheesy Egg and Flax Muffins
Nutrition facts per serving: 130 calories, 8g total fat, 2.5g sat fat, 240mg sodium, 7g total carbohydrate, 3g dietary fiber, 1g sugars, 11g protein

This recipe is inspired by my favorite take-out sandwich from Starbucks®. I know when I'm shopping in the mall, this nutrient packed wrap will save me from the perils of the food court any time of the day. It's also great when traveling because I know I'll at least find whole grains, protein, veggies and fiber. Now you can make this at home and ahead of time. Wrap it up and reheat when you are ready to eat. Pair it with a piece of fruit for a perfectly balanced meal.

SPINACH, EGG WHITE AND FETA WRAP WITH SUN-DRIED TOMATOES —
Makes 1 Serving

Ingredients:
1/4 cup plus 2 Tablespoons liquid egg whites or 2 large egg whites
Small handful of fresh spinach
2 Tablespoons sun-dried tomatoes (not in liquid)
1/4 cup crumbled feta cheese, loosely packed
1 whole grain tortilla (80 calories)

Instructions:
Spray an omelet pan with nonstick spray and heat on medium-high heat.
Add egg whites, tilting the pan to even them out and cook until set.
Add spinach, sun-dried tomatoes, and feta in the middle of the egg whites and fold in half, cooking until cheese melts.
Remove from pan and place on the wrap. Roll wrap around eggs and serve.

Spinach, Egg White and Feta Wrap with Sun-Dried Tomatoes
Nutrition facts per serving: 230 calories, 8g total fat, 3.5g sat fat, 770mg sodium, 26g total carbohydrate, 8g dietary fiber, 6g sugars, 23g protein

Chapter 5:
FUN WITH FRUIT, CEREAL AND ANCIENT GRAINS

Carbs get a bad rap in the media yet they are an important and enjoyable part of a healthy diet. When talking about "good" carbs like fruit and whole grains, the portion is the key for weight management and diabetes. We certainly want the benefit of the key nutrients they provide, just not too much when watching weight and blood sugar. These recipes are indulgent and fun, yet they fit easily into my criteria for a balanced breakfast.

Sorghum may be a "new to you" grain but it's actually an ancient grain that's grown in the USA. It has the size and look of Israeli couscous with the texture of a wheat berry. Sorghum has a gentle bite and doesn't get soggy which means it's ideal to cook in advance and reheat or freeze for later. Sorghum is gluten free and non-GMO if that is important to you, it also requires less water to grow making it a sustainable grain for the future. It's available in many different forms including whole grain or pearled (where the outer hull is removed for quicker cooking but contains less protein and fiber), as well as sorghum flour and sorghum syrup which resembles molasses. For variety, the following Pomegranate Strawberry Sorghum Parfait can also be enjoyed with quinoa, farro, freekeh, brown rice or almost any other ancient grain.

Crepes make me think of my grandma's kitchen on a Saturday morning. She would sauté hers with a bit too much butter and spread grape or strawberry jelly on top. While I miss that sweet treat, my version is filled with fiber rich berries and creamy ricotta for a fancy weekend breakfast to share.

BERRIES AND CREAM FILLED PROTEIN CREPES —
Makes 6 Filled Crepes/2 servings

Ingredients:
Crepes:
1/2 cup unsweetened vanilla almond milk
1 egg
1 egg white or 3 Tablespoons liquid egg whites
2 Tablespoons vanilla whey protein powder
1/4 cup white whole wheat flour

Filling:
1 cup low fat or fat free ricotta cheese
1-2 teaspoons fresh lemon juice
2 packets stevia or preferred sweetener
1-2 teaspoons lemon zest
1 cup fresh blackberries
8 fresh strawberries, stem removed and thinly sliced (about 1.5 cups)

Instructions:
1. In a medium bowl, combine all crepe ingredients and whisk well until combined. You may also blend ingredients in a blender or food processor.
2. Heat a flat round skillet or omelet pan over medium heat. Spray with nonstick cooking spray (I used coconut oil spray).
3. Fill a 1/4 cup measuring cup about 3/4 full of crepe batter and pour in the center of pan/skillet and lift and turn so batter spreads to create a thinner crepe.
4. When bubbles form, turn crepe and cook on other side until golden.
5. Remove from heat, placing on a plate and set aside.
6. Repeat for remaining batter to make 6 crepes.

BERRIES AND CREAM FILLED PROTEIN CREPES – Continued

To make the filling:
In a bowl, combine ricotta, lemon juice, stevia and lemon zest.

To assemble crepes:
Place one crepe on a plate and line with 1/6 of ricotta mixture and 1/6 of the berries. Roll up and repeat for 5 remaining crepes.
If desired, garnish with additional berries and lemon zest.

Tips: To help create a seal, use a very small amount of ricotta mixture on the end of the crepe so it will adhere when rolled up.
If you love lemon, use the higher recommended amount of juice and zest in the ricotta mixture, otherwise, use less to start, you can always add more.

Berries and Cream Filled Protein Crepes
Nutrition facts per serving: 300 calories, 8g total fat, 3g sat fat, sodium, 36g total carbohydrate, 10g dietary fiber, 17g sugars, 27g protein

Switch up your breakfast routine by cooking up different varieties of whole grains. This whole grain sorghum is gluten free and has a chewy texture. It never gets soggy so you can cook a batch ahead of time and keep it in the fridge until you are ready to use it or freeze it to defrost as needed. Layer with your favorite flavor of Greek yogurt and fruit for a hearty, protein and fiber rich meal.

POMEGRANATE STRAWBERRY SORGHUM PARFAIT — Makes 1 Serving

Ingredients:
1/2 cup cooked whole grain sorghum
2 Tablespoons unsweetened vanilla almond milk
1/8 teaspoon vanilla extract
1/2 packet stevia or preferred sweetener
5.3 ounce cup lower sugar strawberry Greek yogurt
1/2 teaspoon hemp seeds or 1 teaspoon ground flax meal
1/3 cup pomegranate seeds

Instructions:
Reheat cooked sorghum with 2 Tablespoons almond milk until warm. Stir in 1/8 teaspoon vanilla extract and 1/2 packet of sweetener.
Place 1/2 of the sorghum in the bottom of a bowl or Mason jar.
Add 1/2 of the yogurt on top of the sorghum.
Top with 1/2 of the pomegranate seeds.
Add remaining sorghum and yogurt.
Sprinkle with hemp or flax seed and pomegranate seeds.
This recipe can be served warm or cold.

Pomegranate Strawberry Sorghum Parfait
Nutrition facts per serving: 300 calories, 2.5g total fat, 0g sat fat, 90mg sodium, 51g total carbohydrate, 12g dietary fiber, 15g sugars, 20g protein

Chocolate covered cherries have always been one of my favorite treats. Why not wake up to this lovely flavor combo in the form of breakfast ice cream? If you are lucky enough to have fresh cherries in season, it's even better.

CHOCOLATE CHERRY BREAKFAST ICE CREAM — Makes 1 Serving

Ingredients:
1/2 cup part-skim ricotta cheese
1/4 cup chocolate whey protein powder
1 Tablespoon unsweetened cocoa powder
1/2-1 packet stevia
10 frozen cherries (about 1/2 cup), defrosted and quartered, reserving the juice.
1/2 teaspoon cacao nibs or mini chocolate chips

Instructions:
Remove cherries from the juice, dice and set aside.
Blend ricotta, protein powder, cocoa powder, stevia and reserved juice from cherries (2-3 teaspoons) in a small food processor or blender until smooth.
Transfer mixture to a bowl and gently stir in cherries.
Place in a serving bowl, top with cacao nibs/ mini chips and refrigerate overnight. Place in freezer in the morning for 15-30 minutes if you prefer a thicker texture. If consuming immediately, place in freezer for 30-45 minutes and enjoy.

Chocolate Cherry Breakfast Ice Cream
Nutrition facts per serving: 300 calories, 11g total fat, 6g sat fat, 260mg sodium, 23g total carbohydrate, 4g dietary fiber, 16g sugars, 34g protein

Cereal has always been a quintessential breakfast food. As a kid, I always craved the sugary cereals I saw on TV but my mom refused to buy. Now you can enjoy the sweet cereal flavor you want without adding sugar, and the addition of protein powder will prevent the mid-morning hunger pangs you might experience after a typical cereal bowl that's too low in protein.

RASPBERRY COCONUT PROTEIN CEREAL BOWL — Makes 1 Serving

Ingredients:
1 cup whole grain puffed cereal (such as Kix™)
1/3 cup high fiber cereal (such as Fiber One™)
3/4 cup unsweetened coconut milk
3 Tablespoons coconut whey protein powder (or vanilla if you cannot find coconut)
1/2 cup raspberries, fresh or frozen (defrosted)
2 teaspoons unsweetened coconut flakes

Instructions:
Add cereal to a serving bowl.
Whisk together protein powder and milk in a large measuring cup or glass.
Add most of the raspberries to cereal and toss, reserving a few for garnish.
Pour milk over the cereal, add remaining berries and coconut flakes to serve.

Raspberry Coconut Protein Cereal Bowl
Nutrition facts per serving: 300 calories, 8g total fat, 7g sat fat, 250mg sodium, 41g total carbohydrate, 11g dietary fiber, 8g sugars, 20g protein

Cereal and yogurt are a perfect pairing. You have creamy meeting crunchy and the addition of bananas adds fiber and sweetness. Combining a few different cereals also creates an interesting texture and you can easily switch up your fruit choice to take advantage of what's in season.

BANANA, YOGURT AND CEREAL BOWL — Makes 1 Serving

Ingredients:
1/3 cup high fiber cereal (like Fiber One™)
1/2 cup whole grain puffed wheat or puffed brown rice cereal
1/2 cup toasted oats cereal (like Cheerios™)
1/2 cup plain, nonfat Greek yogurt
2 Tablespoons vanilla whey protein
1/3 medium banana thinly sliced
(Optional: 1/2 packet stevia)

Instructions:
Combine all the cereals in a bowl and mix.
Stir protein powder into the yogurt and gently fold into the cereal.
Add sliced banana on top or layer in a parfait glass for serving.

Tip: If you are used to sweeter yogurt, add 1/2 packet of stevia with the protein powder before adding the cereal.

Banana, Yogurt and Cereal Bowl
Nutrition facts per serving: 290 calories, 3.5g total fat, .5g sat fat, 200mg sodium, 43g total carbohydrate, 10g dietary fiber, 12g sugars, 28g protein

If increasing fiber is one of your goals, this gem is a winner. Similar to overnight oats, combining high fiber cereal with milk, yogurt and fruit and letting it soak overnight brings a fun texture along with the bright flavors of orange and cranberry. With 20 grams of fiber, this breakfast alone provides 80% of the daily recommended fiber for women!

CLEMENTINE CRANBERRY OVERNIGHT CEREAL BOWL — Makes 1 Serving

Ingredients:
1/2 cup slightly rounded high fiber cereal (30 grams) (like Fiber One™)
2 Tablespoons vanilla whey protein
1 teaspoon chia seeds
1 packet stevia or preferred sweetener
1 teaspoon clementine/mandarin zest
1/3-1/2 cup unsweetened vanilla almond, cashew or coconut milk
1/3 cup nonfat, plain Greek yogurt
2 clementines/mandarins – approximately 4 ounces when peeled, divided
1 Tablespoon (10 grams) dried cranberries

Instructions:
In a bowl or container with a lid, add cereal, whey protein, chia, stevia, zest, milk and yogurt and stir well to combine.
Peel the clementines/mandarins and slice ONE so that each wedge is cut into thirds. Add to mixture and stir. Save the other clementine for topping.
Cover and let sit in the refrigerator for several hours or overnight.
When ready to serve, add slices from the second clementine and 1 Tablespoon of dried cranberries. Layer in a parfait glass or jar if desired.

Tip: If trying to reduce sugar even further, use reduced sugar dried cranberries.

Clementine Cranberry Overnight Cereal Bowl
Nutrition facts per serving: 270 calories, 4g total fat, 0g sat fat, 260mg sodium, 53g total carbohydrate, 20g dietary fiber, 20g sugars, 22g protein

Chapter 6:
SAVORY TOAST AND WRAPS

These days, toast is not just for butter anymore. With tasty toppings such as avocado and sausage, whole grain toast can be beautiful and exciting.

The same goes for wraps as the filling possibilities are endless. No need to wait for the weekend to enjoy smoked salmon, any day of the week will do with a grab and go wrap.

There are so many varieties of wraps available with calories ranging from 60 to well over 200! Most of my recipes are made with wraps ranging from 60-120 calories depending on the recipe type and texture I'm trying to achieve. I tried to leave a little leeway to allow for differences in availability of brands. Find one you like and compare the nutritionals, always aiming for a high amount of protein and fiber vs total calories.

The Protein-Packed Breakfast Club

BONUS WEB RECIPE

PB and Banana "Sushi" recipe available at www.NutritionStarringYOU.com

Avocado toast is a perfect food combination. The pleasantly mild flavor of the avocado over crispy toast is so creamy and satisfying. Add a bit of heat with spicy sausage and it's a flavor explosion. There are so many varieties of sausage that this dish never gets boring, try them all!

AVOCADO TOAST WITH SPICY SAUSAGE — Makes 1 Serving

Ingredients:
2 slices "light" whole wheat bread or whole grain bread of choice (40-45 calories each)
2 ounces avocado, about 1/4 cup, mashed
1 link chicken or turkey sausage that contains 100-140 calories with 11-15 grams of protein
Red pepper flakes to taste

Instructions:
Toast the bread to desired darkness.
Meanwhile, slice the sausage link into thin coin shapes (about 18 slices) and brown on both sides in a sauté pan.
Once toast is done, top with mashed avocado and sausage coins.
Garnish with red pepper flakes

Tips: For a quicker prep, place sausage coins on a plate and microwave for 1 1/2 minutes.
Use any flavor sausage, the nutrition information includes one with 130 calories and 15 grams of protein per link

Avocado Toast with Spicy Sausage
Nutrition facts per serving: 300 calories, 16g total fat, 3g sat fat, 640mg sodium, 24g total carbohydrate, 10g dietary fiber, 2g sugars, 22g protein

Ever since I was a little kid, I have loved bagels and lox (smoked salmon). I remember watching my grandma very sparingly scrape tiny pieces of the freshly sliced lox from the deli paper as she delicately placed it on a toasted frozen bagel. It was one of my favorite sleepover treats, however, as an adult I'm not a fan of the 300-500 calories found in our modern bagels so I've created a way to enjoy my lox and schmears with fewer carbs and calories.

SMOKED SALMON WRAP — Makes 1 Serving

Ingredients:
1 high fiber tortilla wrap (60-80 calories)
1 Tablespoon light cream cheese
2 ounces smoked salmon
1 Campari tomato, sliced
8 slices cucumber

Instructions:
Lay wrap flat and spread cream cheese along center from end to end, reserving a small amount to seal the wrap.
Add smoked salmon, tomato and cucumber slices.
Roll as tightly as possible to keep filling from falling out of wrap, spread remaining cream cheese on the exposed outer edge to help create a seal.
Slice in half and serve.

Tip: If smoked salmon is a staple for you, try to find a nitrate-free version. Also, this recipe is higher in sodium than most. If you have health issues requiring you to limit the sodium in your diet, only enjoy it once in a while.

Smoked Salmon Wrap
Nutrition facts per serving: 220 calories, 11g total fat, 2.5g sat fat, 1030mg sodium, 19g total carbohydrate, 8g dietary fiber, 5g sugars, 20g protein

References

1. Madonna M. Mamerow, Joni A. Mettler, Kirk L. English, et al. Dietary Protein Distribution Positively Influences 24-h Muscle Protein Synthesis in Healthy Adults. J Nutr. 2014 Jun; 144(6): 876–880 doi: 10.3945/jn.113.185280

2. Symons TB, Sheffield-Moore M, Wolfe RR, Paddon-Jones D. A moderate serving of high-quality protein maximally stimulates skeletal muscle protein synthesis in young and elderly subjects. J Am Diet Assoc. 2009 Sep;109(9):1582-6. doi: 10.1016/j.jada.2009.06.369

3. Layman DK. Dietary guidelines should reflect new understandings about adult protein needs. Nutr Metab (Lond). 2009; 6: 12. doi: 10.1186/1743-7075-6-12

4. Brikou D, Zannidi D, Karfopoulou E, Anastasiou CA, Yannakoulia M. Breakfast consumption and weight-loss maintenance: results from the MedWeight study. Br J Nutr. 2016;115(12):2246-2251.

5. O'Neil CE, Byrd-Bredbenner C, Hayes D, Jana L, Klinger SE, Stephenson-Martin S. The role of breakfast in health: definition and criteria for a quality breakfast. J Acad Nutr Diet. 2014;114(12 Suppl):S8-S26.

6. Wyatt HR, Grunwald GK, Mosca CL, Klem ML, Wing RR, Hill JO. Long-term weight loss and breakfast in subjects in the National Weight Control Registry. Obesity. 2002;10(2):78-82.

7. Fallaize R, Wilson L, Gray J, Morgan LM, Griffin BA. Variation in the effects of three different breakfast meals on subjective satiety and subsequent intake of energy at lunch and evening meal. Eur J Nutr. 2013;52(4):1353-1359.

8. Chowdhury EA, Richardson JD, Holman GD, Tsintzas K, Thompson D, Betts JA. The causal role of breakfast in energy balance and health: a randomized controlled trial in obese adults. Am J Clin Nutr. 2016;103(3):747-756.

9. Neumann BL, Dunn A, Johnson D, Adams JD, Baum JI. Breakfast macronutrient composition influences thermic effect of feeding and fat oxidation in young women who habitually skip breakfast. Nutrients. 2016;8(8):490.

10. St-Onge MP, Ard J, Baskin ML, et al. Meal timing and frequency: implications for cardiovascular disease prevention: a scientific statement from the American Heart Association. Circulation. 2017;135(9):e96-e121.

11. Levitsky DA, Pacanowski CR. Effect of skipping breakfast on subsequent energy intake. Physiol Behav. 2013;119:9-16.

12. Jakubowicz D, Barnea M, Wainstein J, Froy O. High caloric intake at breakfast vs. dinner differentially influences weight loss of overweight and obese women. Obesity (Silver Spring). 2013;21(12):2504-2512.

13. Paddon-Jones D, Westman E, Mattes RD, Wolfe RR, Astrup A, Westerterp-Plantenga M. Protein, weight management, and satiety. Am J Clin Nutr. 2008;87(5):1558S-1561S.

14. Paddon-Jones D, Rasmussen BB. Dietary protein recommendations and the prevention of sarcopenia. Curr Opin Clin Nutr Metab Care. 2009;12(1):86-90.

15. Veldhorst MA, Nieuwenhuizen AG, Hochstenbach-Waelen A, et al. Dose-dependent satiating effect of whey relative to casein or soy. Physiol Behav. 2009;96(4-5):675-682.

16. Crowder CM, Neumann BL, Baum JI. Breakfast protein source does not influence postprandial appetite response and food intake in normal weight and overweight young women. J Nutr Metab. 2016;2016:6265789.

The Protein-Packed Breakfast Club

Made in the USA
Middletown, DE
23 December 2017